Parenting Teenage Boys:

How to Raise Your Teen Son During His Adolescent Period Guide

By

Eva Delano

Table of Contents

Introduction 5

Chapter 1. General Principles of Bringing Up an Adolescent Boy 7

Chapter 2. Roles of Parents and How They Should Act 10

Chapter 3. How to Deal with Hormonal Changes of Son and Emotions 14

Chapter 4. Communication 17

Chapter 5. Responsibility and Discipline 20

Chapter 6. Teenage Risks 23

Conclusion 28

Thank You Page 30

Parenting Teenage Boys: How to Raise Your Teen Son During His Adolescent Period Guide

By Eva Delano

© Copyright 2015 Eva Delano

Reproduction or translation of any part of this work beyond that permitted by section 107 or 108 of the 1976 United States Copyright Act without permission of the copyright owner is unlawful. Requests for permission or further information should be addressed to the author.

This publication is designed to provide accurate and authoritative information in regard to the subject matter covered. This work is sold with the understanding that the publisher is not engaged in rendering legal, accounting, or other professional services. If legal advice or other expert assistance is required, the services of a competent professional person should be sought.

First Published, 2015

Printed in the United States of America

Introduction

A teenager refers to someone in their teen age, mostly between the ages of ten to nineteen years. Teenage parenting refers to parental care offered to adolescents. During puberty, boys, as well as girls, undergo physical changes, which may include broadening of chests, deep voices, a growth of pubic hair and increased body growth. However, apart from these changes, boys also undergo through unobservable changes in their body, such as changes in behavior, attitudes, thoughts, social codes and actions. These are termed adolescent changes. Adolescence is a crucial stage in boy child growth and requires a lot of input in parental care. These changes during adolescents may be drastic, boys may act too violently due to high levels of androgens which greatly amplifies anger, and may become indiscipline, disobedient, and irresponsible. These changes may negatively affect boy's life, and as such, a voluminous workload is heaped on the parent to offer good care and support to the teenage boy.

Parents, therefore should highly concentrate on offering comprehensive advice and control of their son's behavior to avoid getting into dangerous behavior and situations.

Chapter 1. General Principles of Bringing Up an Adolescent Boy

During an adolescent period, a parent should be understanding and aware of the changes that take place in the boy's life. As such, a parent should acquaint themselves with knowledge on possible expected behavioral changes, from online resources, print or electronic media.

Parents should be close to their son. A good parent should not abandon or stay too far away from the son, because monitoring is required to keep the son's behavior in check, to observe his activities, correct where he seems wrong and congratulate where he has done perfectly. This modeling, which is a prerequisite in responsible upbringing, will promote the son's activities towards doing what is rewarding and avoiding what is not rewarding. Also, parents should speak and advise their sons accordingly. Teenage boys deal with problems better if they have prior information on what they will be going through. They also make wise choices on informed decisions. This a springboard to a positive behavior growth. Moreover, being free with teenage sons when talking would help in revealing their heightened fears, and this revelation would be very helpful in advising them and parenting them.

Modeling is also another way of responsibly bringing up children. Responsible parents have the advantage of having responsible children, because the children vicariously learn from their parents. This passively learned experience is paramount in determining the son's behavior and actions. Many children learn to drink alcohol from their parents, which is equally important as learning to smoke. Therefore, sons of parents who don't smoke will probably not smoke. Parents are the first role models and mentors for the sons. Therefore, a bad behavior in a parent will be transferred to the child, and healthy practice will encourage the good behavior of the son too. In addition, sons should be taught about money and how to spend it. Children who don't know how to spent money in the right way mess up with their lives. They are easily prone to drug and alcohol abuse, and sexual immorality, among many other problems.

Parents should be aware of teenage risks. They should have knowledge on how changes of behaviors predispose their adolescent boy to dangers such as sex, drug abuse, bad companies and bad behaviors. They should therefore be ready to deal with such problems, to ensure their son grows up responsibly. If parents have such information, it would be easy for them to understand and deal with the sudden changes in behavior of their sons. This is prerequisite in positively helping their son with advice and education on how to deal with sexual feelings and desires.

Chapter 2. Roles of Parents and How They Should Act

Parents play an important role in ensuring proper growth of a child. Parents provide son's safety. Good security of the son starts with the parent. A good parent should ensure their son doesn't get into harm, either from other people or by engaging in risky situations. Providing education is also another role of a parent. This may be formal or informal. Formal education involves taking a child to school or any other higher learning institution. Informal education involves advising, encouraging and directing the child on life issues such as responsibility, discipline, honesty, truthfulness, and how to perform duties assigned to them. These issues require a great parental involvement to help the son understand their roles, expectations, and above all, fulfill their dreams in life.

A parent is also ought to offer food and shelter to the son. Any parent is required by the constitution to offer adequate food and proper housing for a child. Any inadequacy of these will lead serious consequences. Inadequacy of food may lead the son to engage in dangerous activities such as robbery and violence, engagement in sale of drugs, and alcohol abuse. Moreover, this may lead the son to avoid coming home and hook up with dangerous peers such as drunkards, smokers and drug abusers. Lack of proper shelter may also lead to avoidance of home and lead to involvement in heinous activities such as stealing. It can also predispose a son to diseases such asthma, pneumonia and other respiratory tract infections. A parent should also offer enough clothing to the son. He should mind buying the son enough clothing.

Parents also have a responsibility of letting children take charge of their work. They should show their children that they are responsible of their success and failures. They should show the child motivation to do their work, and encourage them to achieve their set goals and objectives. Parents also have a responsibility of helping their child connect what they learn in school with the real world. Parents should help children visualize theorized school work. For example, parents should help children explain, for example, the effects of drugs with example of personalities who abuse such drugs. With this, he child can connect what they learn and happenings, therefore making a permanent impression of mental picture in his mind. This is important for proper mental development of the son. It is also important for applying issues into a bigger picture in the real world.

Moreover, a parent should always offer advises to their sons on various life issues. They should teach the child on how to behave, how to respond to various challenges in life and how to achieve their dreams. They should always be free with their sons and avoid no issues which may include sexual desires, boyfriends/girlfriend issues and sexuality. They should not evade such issues but discuss profoundly. This will give knowledge the children on how to deal with their emotions and sexual desires and emotions.

Parents should also provide a sense of belonging to the son. They should always hold on to the needs of the son and not use abusive words which may negatively affect the feelings of the son. For example, they should not insult the son in case of wrong doing. A sense of belonging is important in boosting the self-esteem of the son and contribute in positive attitude and good behavior.

Parents should not discriminate against some of their sons but deal with them uniformly. They should advise their sons and warn them when they do wrong. Both parents should take part in talking with the son, so that it will be deemed a massive issue, and the son will take it with a heavy note. This will promote firmness in sticking to such advice. And with a continued adherence to the advice, the son will overcome the intricacies that are associated with adolescence.

Parents should also become role models to their son. They should avoid drinking, or if they do, do it in private to avoid influencing them into drinking alcohol. They should always engage in activities that will impact positively to the behavior of their sons and not to influence it negatively. They should teach their son on requirements of their religious faith on sex and relationship, virtues and values. Parents should also take their sons for counseling sessions, and seminars and peer mentors to help them acquire information on responsibility and importance of living a disciplined and responsible life as an adolescent.

Chapter 3. How to Deal with Hormonal Changes of Son and Emotions

During adolescence, a son goes through hormonal surges, which changes his behavior, attitudes and actions. A boy has higher androgens in his body during adolescence. These androgens handle the male sexual characteristics such as the hoarse voice and broadened chest. However, these changes of hormones bring in changes of behavior and emotions that may not be good.

Parents should always advise their son to regulate anger. High levels of androgen hormones in the body amplify anger, and, therefore many sons get angry during adolescents. Such anger may lead to violence and emotional response to some events. Therefore, parents should advise their son on how to avoid violence. They should encourage him to stay away from annoying events that may provoke his wrath. And in case the son gets angry at the parents in any instance, parents ought to understand him from the knowledge they have that androgens, amplify anger in boys' lives during adolescence.

Parents should also deal with sons' emotions accordingly. They should be there to give support to the son when in deep emotional distress such as when rejected by peers, or when they experience strange happenings in their life such as wet dreams. At such moments, they need parental advice on how to deal and curb dangerous emotional desires such as lust, and how to control these emotions. A parent who has extensive knowledge of such information on an emotional control will abundantly help the son in dealing with his feelings.

Parents should also warn their children on lustful emotions, advising them on dangers of teenage sex such as sexually transmitted diseases, early pregnancies and possible dropout from school, unplanned marriages and parenting responsibilities. They should always help their son to avoid teenage sex, advising him that his time will come in future. They should advise him to concentrate on schoolwork, helping his parents and other people in then society. With such information, the son will acquaint himself with the dangers of premarital sex and avoid it, dealing positively with his emotions.

In addition, parents should also monitor the kind of information their son views in different media. They should control the type of information their son can access from the internet. They should be blocked from accessing erotic information and media in-home Wi-Fi network, and they should be regulated from the program they watch on televisions and time they watch. An allowance of the son to access erotic and pornographic material from the internet will thwart efforts to regulate their sexual desires and will opt for teenage sex. This is a dangerous act as it can lead to the aforementioned consequences such as early marriages and sexually transmitted infections.

Chapter 4. Communication

Communication between a parent and a son should be friendly and not commandeering. This friendly state will promote cooperation and understanding between the parent and son. Understanding is good for mutual respect and cooperation. For revelation of secrets between the son and the parent to occur, they should be open to each other. Openness promotes easiness in passing information, understanding and possible ease in meeting set goals for the son.

Communication should not be that of command/order- and submission. A good parent understands that for the son to have respect and attain set goals, he should own the idea as if it were his. If this is violated, a son's response to a command from the parent will be viewed as an order, and the son will do it just to finish, and not to fulfill everything that is required of him. This way of action is annoying to the son, and as such, he will be bored with the day to day orders to perform certain actions.

Communication that is mutual, that of advice and cooperation, is very healthy. Sons want independence and relief from directions to do something. They want to be free from parental control. They want to own everything pertaining them. Therefore, sons do something excellently if they feel they own an idea, towards a certain action. If the parents advise them to do something, giving them freedom to either do it or omit, and advising them on possible consequences of their choice, sons will be in a better position to perform it with their utmost strength and knowledge. Therefore, sons should be left to choose their direction towards doing something. However, this trust of choice on their part should not be jeopardized, parents should offer limits to this trust of choice accorded to them.

Parents should also ensure regular communications between them and their son. Parents should not only talk to their sons when an issue arises, such as misunderstanding. Regular discussions on issues eliminate suspicions, encourage openness and revelation of secrets.

Good behaviors are inculcated through good and proper communication. In situation where communication is crippled, there will be the most extemporaneous behaviors experienced. They will not have any directions on what is expected of them, how to behave and it will cripple relationship with the son and friends, and with the son and the parents. Therefore, good communication is very important between the son and the parents to inculcate a positive life growth.

Chapter 5. Responsibility and Discipline

Every child is required to be responsible in their work as a duty towards their parents. Responsibility and discipline is a sign of respect and obedience to parents. It's a parents' right to be respected by any child. However, during adolescents, boys may become rude, get angry easily, and may be violent towards their parents. This behavior may be annoying to the parents. Therefore, proper behavior should be inculcated to make them responsible and disciplined.

Parents should monitor their son's friends and friends' friends. This is very important, as peer influence is paramount in determining a son's behavior. Parents should go to the extent of knowing their son's friends' parents. For better and proper behavior, parents should encourage their son to have friends with the same goal, and not those with extemporaneous behavior. They should encourage their son to avoid friends who smoke, drink or take any drugs, as their son would be influenced into such heinous behavior.

To teach their son responsibility, a parent should set goals for the son. For example, set his target in exams based on prior performance, and reward the son on attainment of the set goal. This is important to encourage the son do more and aim higher. Continuous setting of goals and rewarding will teach the son responsibility throughout his life.

Parents should also expect their adolescent son to help them in household chores during holidays and whenever they are at home. A son who helps parent with daily chores will learn how to do some actions, and will use the knowledge learned to apply when there is no one to help them, for example when they become independent they can cook for themselves.

To inculcate discipline, a parent should punish a child on wrongdoing. The parent should lucidly explain to the son what and how he has done wrong, the consequences of the wrongdoing and justify what he should be punished. Punishment should not be too violent, that will injure the son. Injurious punishment will make the son violent. Rewarding good actions also inculcates discipline. Sons who are rewarded tend to do more actions that are rewarding and avoid those that are not rewarding. Reward will promote doing what is right and avoid what is wrong, which promotes discipline.

Also, parents should always ensure their sons are occupied. They should not give them a voluminous free time, or give them too much time for watching television, play computer games or browse the web. Parents should set time for certain actions, so that the sons are not always idle. An idle mind will give in to many intriguing activities such as alcohol abuse, drugs, and sexual activities. Giving them expectations on time they should be done with certain activities is a good way to teach them responsibility and punctuality in duties. With such, the sons will learn to perform their work on time and avoid delays.

Parents should also understand the importance of school in inculcating discipline and responsibility. Parents should advise their son to always respect his teachers and do what they say and what is according to school rules and regulations. They should allow their son to be reprimanded in case of wrongdoing, to plant a behavior of discipline, responsibility and honesty. They should therefore work closely with teachers to keep their son's behavior in check.

Chapter 6. Teenage Risks

Teens go through a lot of risks in their teen lives. The risks range from those that are not very dangerous to those that are too dangerous to practice.

Alcoholism is one of the risks that teens get introduction to during adolescence. They are mostly brought in by having excess money such a pocket money, peer influence and other risks such as abundance of bars and drinking places. Consumption of alcohol is regulated by the government, prohibiting sale of alcohol to people of certain age. However, some teens still get their way to buy this alcohol. This is a risk that affects many adolescent sons. Alcohol consumption negatively affects school work performance, increases risks of having uncontrolled sex, getting into violence and engaging in unlawful activities. This is a risk that affects many adolescent boys in the world, and has led to drastic bad effects. Therefore, parents should be more cautious when dealing with their sons to prevent them from alcohol consumption and avoid possible bad consequences.

In addition, teenage sex is also a chief risk in teenage lives. During adolescents, boys discover their sexual feelings, and this discovery increases sexual desires. This increases risks of getting predisposed to sexually transmitted infections such as HIV/AIDS, syphilis, gonorrhea, and chancroid, just to mention a few. The effects of these diseases are heinous, some such as AIDS leading to death, while others may cause brain damage, infertility and may even cause death, if medical intervention is not sought earlier. Parents should talk with their son to discover their sexual feelings, desires and use the knowledge to advise their son accordingly. However, the parents should not be too close to their son that they jeopardize his privacy. They should allow personal space, and create room for privacy for their son.

Drug abuse is also another risk many teenagers go through. Abuse of hard drugs such as heroin, cocaine and Cannabis sativa is a major problem affecting the contemporary society. The effects of urbanization, easy transport and online purchases and cashless payments have aided in purchase, distribution, sales and deliveries of these drugs. This has eased access to such drugs among the youth, and increased abuse, making it a worldwide problem, causing worldwide outcry for interventions. Therefore, parents should advise their sons on drugs, their effects and factors that predispose one to the abuse of such drugs. Early teenage drug awareness aids in averting predilection to abuse of drugs. The community, government officials, religious institutions and school should make special efforts in disseminating information on dangers of drug abuse. These institutions can act as places for counseling adolescent boys and their peers. If such plans are made, the war and fight against drug and alcohol abuse will be one of victory, and is a springboard to better parenting and better inculcation of positive behavior when it comes to the upbringing of an adolescent boy. Therefore, parents, schools and the community should work together in molding a boy's behavior.

Another risk that adolescents may also go through is separation in search of independence. Many adolescent boys start living an isolated life, some may migrate to urban centers searching for jobs, and others may demand to live on their own. Most of these occurrences occur mostly when the boy has dropped out of school. With such requirements, most of them are allowed to live on their own, and they get out of parental control. They are therefore free to do what they wish to do, many of them engaging in alcohol and drug abuse, teenage sex and relationship, and smoking. These factors are risky and the parents should consider it wise to help them get out of their freedom of isolation and independence.

Adolescents also have a risk of being influenced by ads, for example, they can easily give in to smoking when they see cigarette advertisements. They can also be changed easily into a particular habit, dressing code, or particular event. Therefore, parental advice is required for discretion between good and bad choices. In case of advertisements such as those of alcohol and cigarettes, parents should be explaining to their sons the impacts of such drugs on health. They should explain their side effects, and how it will socially and economically affect his life. The parents should explicitly encourage their son not to drink or smoke.

Another teenage risk is stress. Most teens get stressed on day to day issues, in case they don't face in what they are doing, or in case they are rejected by their friends. Stress is a significant mental problem and may lead to other problems such as hypertension and high blood pressure. Stress among adolescent boys may be so acute, and may have a profound underlying problem. In case of rejection by friends, betrayal of love, and lack of enough money, many teen boys may be so stressed that they may take away their lives. They may opt to suicide when they see their future opaque, with no optimism, that their dreams will not come true. At such times, they see suicide as the only solution to forget their problems. At such instance, parental care is highly recommended. Moreover, parents should involve professional counselors to help guide him to avoid suicidal feelings.

Conclusion

Many lives are lost to dictations of adolescents, ranging from alcoholism, drug abuse, teenage sex, anger leading to violence and disrespect to parents. These effects are discouraging, and are heinous. Many parents experience a period of lost hopes on the part of their son's expectations during adolescence. Many school dropouts are adolescent boys, or dropped out of school when they were adolescent. Therefore, adolescence is a period of both physical, mental, attitude and goal changes. It's a period that requires the more parental involvement, advice, understanding, and perseverance. It is a period of attitude change on part of the parent, not to be too violent towards the adolescent boy who goes through uncontrollable changes in his body which are normal. Therefore, parents should involve themselves in ensuring their son grows to become a useful member of the society, by guiding them to have and attain set proper goals, by acting in schoolwork, being responsible, obedient, and truthful, honest and disciplined. Parental advice is necessary for the son to maneuver through life's intricacies and challenges. With the right advice, encouragements, friends, and freedom, an adolescent boy will grow up to be a responsible man, going through failures and overcoming many intriguing life challenges. It is very difficult to help successfully a son get out of adolescence without a failure on his part; therefore parents should have a wide knowledge to help them deal with adolescent boys well. This will be a springboard to an attainment of parental goals on parenthood, care and security to their boy child. It is a chance to fully wrap up a child's behavior into a whole, one that is according to societal norms and standards of discipline, one that respects and believes in doing what is right and avoiding what is wrong.

Parental care is critical in positive child upbringing. It is important in inculcating good moral values, and coaching a son to have the desired behavior, which will enable him to become a useful and responsible citizen in contributing to nation building.

Thank You Page

I want to personally thank you for reading my book. I hope you found information in this book useful and I would be very grateful if you could leave your honest review about this book. I certainly want to thank you in advance for doing this.

If you have the time, you can check my other books too.

www.ingramcontent.com/pod-product-compliance
Lightning Source LLC
LaVergne TN
LVHW021747060526
838200LV00052B/3520